BATTLE OF GETTYSBURG

FOR KIDS

CHARLES MCKINNEY

BATTLE OF GETTYSBURG

History of Most Influential Battle of Gettysburg

FOR KIDS

CHARLES MCKINNEY

DR. HISTORY

Don't Forget Your Free Bonus Downloads!

As our way of saying thank you, we've included in every purchase bonus gift downloads. If you've enjoyed reading this book, please consider leaving a review.

Or Scan Your Phone to open QR code

Battlle of Gettysburg:

History of Most Influential Battle of Gettysburg for Kids

Copyright © 2023 by Dr. History

Battle of Gettysburg

TABLE OF CONTENTS

Battle of Gettysburg

INTRODUCTION

"All men are created equal."

- Abraham Lincoln (The Gettysburg Address)

War is something that has been going on for centuries since the beginning of time. Different wars in different countries, eras of time, and between which peoples have started for a multitude of reasons. Sometimes wars are fought because of territory and land. There are other times when wars are fought because of resources. There were wars that were caused by a revolution and a rebellion. There were wars fought because of a demand in different supplies and resources. There was even one war that took place centuries ago where it was believed that two nations went head-to-head all because of a beautiful woman.

In the heat of battle, many fight in wars for the gold, the glory, and the fame. In a time of peace, many idolize the heroes who fought in these wars, yet forget what the cost was in order for these people to be deemed heroic. Many forget about the lives that had to be sacrificed and lost in order to win a battle for territory, beliefs, resources, and whatever possible reason there could be to start a war.

The American Civil War was a war fought between the country's federal government against a group of rebels who wanted to keep living the way they have been living, they wanted to keep their slaves and keep the slave trade alive. They believed that the country should be run solely by the ways of the Christian beliefs.

It was during the height of the American Civil War, a war of one country between two factions who each had their own beliefs of how they wanted their country to be run, held one of the deadliest battles in American history. This battle is known as the Battle of Gettysburg. It was a battle between the Confederacy and the Union that spanned a total of three days, all because two warring sides just happened to chance upon each other just right on the outskirts of a small town. Yet, even without preparation, no rest from the battles they had just fought, no mercy or hesitance was initially shown from either side, and instead, the moment the two warring sides laid eyes on each other, immediately swung their swords and fired their guns.

SLAVERY IN AMERICA

The photograph shows an aerial view of a battle reenactment
of the Battle of Gettysburg. This photograph was taken in 1922.

Slavery in the United States of America started in 1526 even before the United States was colonized by Britain. When the United States were first being occupied by European countries and were thus being colonized by them, there was a great demand for labor. The demand for labor comes from the construction of new buildings, houses, towns, as well as needing workers to work in plantation sites. In these plantation sites, it is somewhat like a farm except it is a vast land overseen by the master of the house, who is usually a slave owner. The land is also large enough to house the slaves who worked in these plantation sites. Slaves were used to take care of livestock and harvest crops.

In the Americas, the first area to be enslaved was the Caribbean. Christopher Columbus first claimed the Caribbean for Spain, which paved the way for Spanish settlements to be made in the land. Years later, Caribbean will then be colonized by other European countries such as Britain and France.

The existence of sugar was what made the Caribbean so special to these countries, making them an easy objective to win wars and land disputes. Over time, many of these countries settled into the Caribbean, South America, and other states in North and Central America, and most of those who settled here had put up their own plantation sites. Because the many decided that they would put up their own plantations, the demand for slaves grew and grew, yet the number of natives had diminished due to the many wars and battles that were fought by the Europeans to claim land. Though slavery wasn't new to the Natives themselves, it was different now that foreigners had taken over and were enslaving pretty much everyone they saw.

Meanwhile, sometime in the 15th century, the Portuguese had an expedition to find India. Sometime in their search, they had found the Kongo Kingdom, now known as Northern Angola in central Africa. At the time, it was just a brief stopover during their search, but was a valuable piece of information much later during the need for more slaves. The constant migration of Europeans to the Americas meant that there was a great need for slaves. This had become the start of the Atlantic Slave Trade, also known as the "Euro-American Slave Trade."

In the 16th century, the Portuguese saw an opportunity. With the demand for slaves getting higher and higher, they had gone back to Africa and brought Africans to the Americas as slaves to be presented and sold to the highest bidders. The Africans they brought back with them to turn into slaves were not there of their own free will. Most were kidnapped or captured in battle. Others were turned into slaves as punishment. There were also some Africans who took the upper hand and made a business out of capturing slaves from other tribes or groups and sold them to the Europeans. Because there was such a high mortality rating for the Africans, there was always a demand for more Africans to use as slaves.

The reason why the mortality rating was so high starts from how they were acquired in the first place. Again, many were there not because of their own volition. Next, was the transportation from Africa to America. Hundreds if not thousands of Africans were chained together and forced to stay together on a ship where they would struggle to survive for the months that it would take to reach America. If they didn't die from the poor and unsanitary conditions of the slave ships, there was also the possibility of dying at the hands of a sailor. Because slaves were thought of at the time as no more than property or even objects, those in charge of handling the transportation did not care to act humane or kind to the people they were transporting, thus abuse was inevitable. It has been estimated that around two million Africans died during the trip going to America.

States now known as the Carolinas, Georgia, Florida, Texas, Virginia, New England, New York, and many others were just some of the states that kept a high number of slaves in their lands. As years progressed, the situation for slaves started to turn around. Some colonists had started to see Africans as more than just "slaves" and as actual human beings just like them. Though there was still a bias against them, Africans started gaining rights and laws. Some states even allowed slaves to be paid in wages.

Slavery started out sometime in the 15th century. From Natives to Africans, the Europeans and colonists did their best to make full use of their strength, power, and wealth to their advantage. However, things started to change for Africans sometime in the 19th century, during the American Civil War.

Fun Fact:

Harriet Tubman was a slave who was able to escape from her slave master. She led other slaves to freedom by using the underground railroads as an escape route to the Union camp at Port Royal, South Carolina. She taught freed slave women skills that they could also use to earn wages and live independently. She later assisted the Union Army be being a spy and gaining intelligence about the actions of the Confederacy through other slaves.

Fun Fact:

General Ulysses S. Grant had a reputation for being the general with the most bloodshed during the American Civil War because of the high body counts in every battle that he fought in and led. The body counts were so high that even President Lincoln's wife, Mary Lincoln, called General Grant a "butcher." However, what most did not realize was that General Robert Lee had a much higher body count than General Grant did because he actually enjoyed the battle and conflict.

Trivia Questions:

1. When did slavery start in the United States of America?

2. What were slaves used for that they were such a commodity?

3. What else was the Atlantic Slave Trade known as?

4. Which states kept a large number of slaves in their estates?

5. Who was the former slave who escaped and helped other slaves to escape by using the underground railroad?

Answers:

1. When did slavery start in the United States of America? **1526**

2. What were slaves used for that they were such a commodity? **Slaves were used to take care of livestock and harvest crops**

3. What else was the Atlantic Slave Trade known as? **The Euro-American Slave Trade**

4. Which states kept a large number of slaves in their estates? **The Carolinas, Georgia, Florida, Texas, Virginia, New England, New York**

5. Who was the former slave who escaped and helped other slaves to escape by using the underground railroad? **Harriet Tubman**

THE UNION AND THE CONFEDERATES

The picture is a picture of a painting from the cyclorama of the Battle of Gettysburg

When the American Civil War started, the country was divided into two warring factions: The Union, otherwise known as, "The North," and The Confederacy, otherwise known as, "The South." The main cause of the American Civil War was the topic of slavery. One side fought for the end of slavery, whereas the other side fought to expand slavery into more western states, which would only lead to the rise of slavery in the United States.

The North was also referred to as the United States. They were led by President Abraham Lincoln, who was a Republican of the National Union Party who won the election of 1860. They were named as such because their goal is to preserve America as a "constitutional union," which refers to founding of the formation of the people, as well as to the states of America fighting in unity. They were also known as the "northern states loyal to the American government." The union consisted of twenty free states and five border states.

"Free state" refers to a state in America where slavery is considered to be illegal. On the other hand, "Slave state" is the opposite, meaning it is a state in America where slavery is legal. "Border state" you could say is a mix of the two. Border states are states in America where slavery is still considered to be legal, however they are states that have joined the ranks of the Union.

The Confederacy was a group of states that claimed to have broken free of The Union, however that decision was never officially recognized by The Union itself or any other foreign countries. The Confederacy was originally formed by seven slave states: Texas, Louisiana, Georgia, South Carolina, Florida, Alabama, and Mississippi. Later on, they were joined by more slave states, making up a total of eleven states in the Confederacy. The eleven states that made up the Confederacy were: South Carolina, North Carolina, Mississippi, Florida, Alabama, Georgia, Louisiana, Tennessee, Virginia, Arkansas, and Texas. Though they did not officially join the Confederacy, Kentucky and Missouri both broke away from the Union, and thus were considered a part of the Confederacy for their participation in the Confederate Congress.

The Confederacy was led by Jefferson Davis. He was a Democrat who represented Mississippi in the House of Representatives and in the United States Senate prior to the American Civil War. Also prior to the Civil War, he owned and ran a cotton plantation where he also owned a hundred and thirteen slaves to serve him and provide labor in his plantation.

It is sufficient to say that The Union, being mostly made up of states that are against slavery, had the objective to remove slavery from America once and for all. Because of this, The Union were occasionally referred to as "abolitionists" by the Confederacy. Then there is the Confederacy that still believed in slavery and that the "negros" are not considered human beings, but material possessions, hence why even though there have been new laws passed for the sake of the rights of the African people, they are still considered slaves, nonetheless.

During the war, the Union held the upper hand. The Union had more resources, funding, and manpower. As the war went on, the insufficient funds and resources that the Confederacy had, shrunk and diminished with every passing year of the war. This was one of the factors that led to the eventual victory of the Union.

Most of the soldiers who fought for the Union were volunteers. A lot of the soldiers who fought for the Union, whether they be volunteers or not, were motivated by their political beliefs and how important they perceived liberty to be, and thus wanted to fight for state rights and abolish slavery. There were also others who were motivated by the thought of protecting their family and their home. All these reasons helped the men and their drive to fight during the war.

Just as the Confederacy had first started, Jefferson Davis, whom at the time had yet to be inaugurated as the President of the Confederacy, had put out a call for 100,000 men from various states in order to fight for the Confederacy and defend it. Around this time in early 1861, most of the states that made up the Confederacy were still in the process of secession from the Union, most of whom were denied. At the same time, The Union was holding talks of getting back together as a nation, to which the states vying for secession refused. Jefferson Davis was then officially inaugurated as the Confederate president and thus continued to raise the much-needed army consisting of 100,000 men to fight in the battles to come once the Civil War starts.

Fun Fact:

When conflict was starting to arise in Virginia, General Robert Lee and his wife fled their 1,100-acre estate in Virginia. Their estate was called, Arlington. In 1863, the Union confiscated Arlington and President Abraham Lincoln had their estate converted into a cemetery for those who died in the American Civil War so that if General Lee were to ever return, he would get to see what his actions of war had cost.

Fun Fact:

General Ulysses S. Grant and General Robert E. Lee were both famous generals during the American Civil War due to their prowess in battle, their ability to strategize in the best way they can with the resources and advantages, and disadvantages that they had. Many both dreaded and speculated when the two generals would go head-to-head on the battlefield, which finally happened in May of 1864.

Match Phrases:

Match the god to the relevant phrases about them.

Free State	Another name for the Union who wanted to free slaves and keep the country united.
The North	States that still had slaves but did not leave the Union.
The South	Another name for the Confederacy who wanted to keep slaves and keep the traditional ways of the country.
Slave State	States where slavery is considered illegal.
Border State	States where slavery is considered legal.

Answers:

Match the god to the relevant phrases about them.

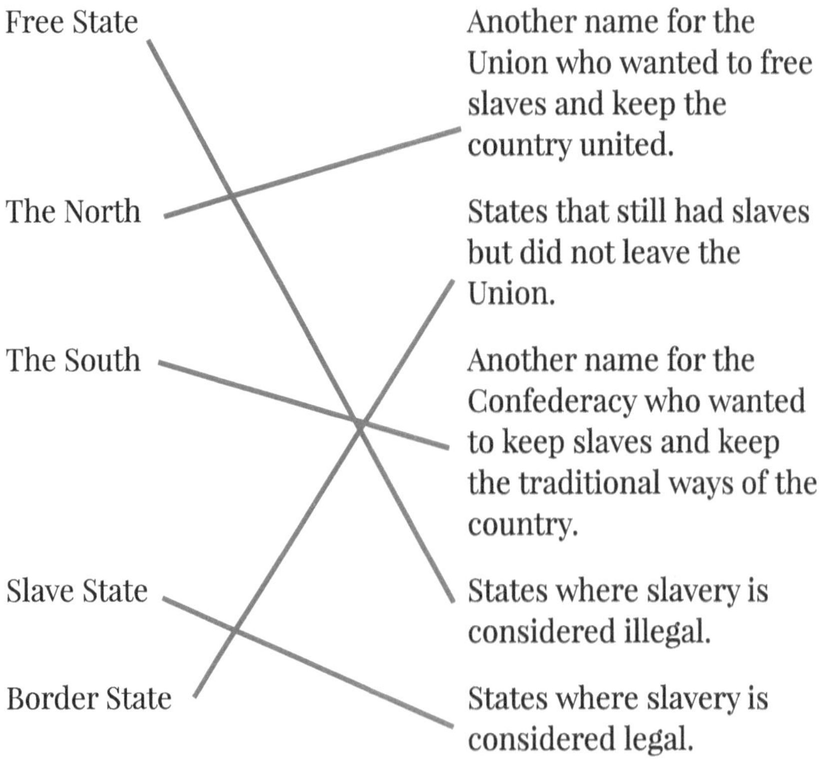

THE CIVIL WAR

The photo is a picture of the 105th Wildcats Regiment Memorial of the Battle of Gettysburg. This is located in the outer corner of the Peach Orchard that was also used as a battlefield during the Battle of Gettysburg.

April 12, 1861 marked the start of the American Civil War when the Confederate Army opened fire on Fort Sumter. Fort Sumter was under the jurisdiction of the Union, but was located in South Carolina, a Confederate state. From the start of the Civil War on April 12, 1861, up until the end of the Civil War on May 26, 1865, it is said that about seven hundred thousand people died. Some of those in this estimate includes both soldiers who fought on either side, and civilians who were all caught in the crossfire. The amount of Americans who died in the Civil War were higher than the number of Americans who died during the American Revolution, World War I, World War II, and even the Vietnam War combined.

The border states, which, again, are slave states that did not leave the Union, played a critical role in helping the Union win against the Confederacy. Maryland was north of the nation's capital, Washington, D.C., Kentucky controlled the Ohio River, and Missouri was the Union's route going to the western states.

At the time of the war, many of the people involved, especially the politicians, denied that slavery was the cause of the war. These people who denied it, kept pushing people to believe that the war was actually because of agriculture, to which many historians have countered that fact, because had the Civil War been about agriculture, then the Civil War would have taken place during the 1830's, which was when the Nullification Crisis took place.

Abraham Lincoln, himself, was one of these politicians who denied that slavery was the actual cause of the war. Abraham

Lincoln stated that his only objective was just to preserve the Union and bring back the states that had seceded. However, other than slavery, many were also motivated by the religious beliefs each side, the Union and the Confederacy, fought for. The Union made it its religious goal to spread Christianity all around the United States, and even to other countries, as well as preserve "God's plan to extend Democracy." The Confederacy, on the other hand, wanted to use the war in order to make a nation more perfect in its fealty to God than the one that they had left. A lot of soldiers who fought in the Civil War were motivated by their religious beliefs. Now, it was believed that the opposite beliefs in religion, slavery, and being united were factors so strongly believed in that it was enough to cause a war within a single nation.

The Civil War ended on April, 1865. It was not a surprise to many that the Union had won the war. From the very beginning, The Union already had a great advantage over the Confederacy in terms of resources, the number of men they had fighting on both sides, and even land. The Union had an estimate of twenty-two thousand men fighting for them, many of whom were volunteers. This many men was a massive advantage over the nine million men that the Confederacy had. It definitely did not help the Confederacy to have three million of their fighting men being slaves, who were obviously not so motivated to fight against people who were trying to abolish slavery.

In terms of resources, The Union was actually manufacturing about ninety percent of the nation's goods. These goods included textiles, shoes, iron, and firearms, all of which were items that were desperately needed in times of war. Additionally, because this was taking place in the nineteenth century, transportation vehicles such as cars, trucks, planes, tanks, and most of what modern society has today had still yet to be invented at the time. However, one of the main modes of transportation that was being used at the time was the train and the railroad tracks. The Union and the Confederacy both used the railroad in order to transport their army, but the railroad tracks were still owned by specific sides of the war. The Confederacy had ten thousand miles worth of railroad tracks under their jurisdiction, yet the Union overpowered them with over twenty miles worth of railroad tracks, making it much easier for them to transport their army.

Though resources and manpower play a very big part in war, or in any event that you could do, one of the major disadvantages of the Confederacy was having to build a nation from scratch. The Union was just as is. Abraham Lincoln's goal was to preserve that union and bring back the states that had left. However, the Confederacy had to build a nation, deal with the class divide, and people who were committed to the autonomy of their individual home states.

Historians estimate that there were about eight thousand acts of violence done between the Union and the Confederacy from 1861 up to 1865. Out of that eight thousand, only fifty of them were considered to be major battles. Some of these major battles were: the First Bull Run in 1861, the Battle of Fort Donelson in 1862, and the Battle of Gettysburg in 1863.

Fun Fact:

The American Civil War officially ended in April of 1865, with victory being celebrated by the Union. Though the Confederates, or the South, rather, were the ones who rebelled and push for war and conflict, they were the ones left bankrupt at the end of the war. Many of its roads, farms, and factories were also left either very damaged, or completely decimated.

Fun Fact:

When the war ended in 1865, the United States later began what was later known as the "Reconstruction Era." This era lasted for twenty long years. The Reconstruction Era actually started in 1863 when many former slaves were freed and had to be integrated into society, but with the added destruction of the American Civil War, the Reconstruction Era lasted until 1877.

Complete the Sentences

1. The American Civil War officially started in April of _____.

2. The American Civil War officially ended in ______ of 1865.

3. Many denied that ________ was the cause of the war.

4. It was not a surprise that the ______ had won the war.

5. The Union was manufacturing over ninety percent of the nation's ______.

Answers:

1. The American Civil War officially started in April of **1861.**

2. The American Civil War officially ended in **April** of 1865.

3. Many denied that **slavery** was the cause of the war.

4. It was not a surprise that the **Union** had won the war.

5. The Union was manufacturing over ninety percent of the nation's **goods.**

RECONNAISSANCE MISSION GONE WRONG

The photo shows Confederate prisoners after the Battle of Gettysburg that was taken in 1863. This photo was originally in black and white, but was later colorized.

On the summer of 1963, the American Civil War had reached a tipping point. Both the Union and the Confederacy have refused to back down from each other, yet both sides were on the verge of a major breakthrough. In 1963, the army of Northern Virginia, which is an army under the Confederacy, was marching up to the state of Pennsylvania under the lead of Robert E. Lee. The army of Northern Virginia was an army of seventy thousand men strong. This was right after they had previously won a series of major victories against the Union.

Robert E. Lee's goal, at this point, was to take over more territories in order to convince the other politicians to sue for peace.

What Robert E. Lee did not know was that the Army of the Potomac, being led by Major General George Meade, was also making its way towards the state of Pennsylvania. The Army of the Potomac was an army of ninety-three thousand men. This army is an army under the Union. They were following Robert E. Lee's army going North ever since they were defeated by the Confederacy in Chancellorsville.

Waging war at this point was neither side's goal, especially after having been fighting battles one after the other for several weeks if not months by now. However, things changed on July 1st of 1963 when both the army of Northern Virginia and the Army of the Potomac all chanced upon each other just right outside of the town of Gettysburg. A few units from the army of Northern Virginia had gone into town in order to get supplies. Once they had reached Gettysburg, they saw the Army of the Potomac stationed just outside of the town. They had immediately gone back to join the rest of the army in order to inform them of the presence of the Confederal Cavalry. Henry Hill, one of the provisional commanders, had initially not believed the report. Two divisions of the army were then sent off with the order to determine the size of the Union's cavalry the next day.

The generals of the army of Northern Virginia were convinced that the cavalry that was spotted was only a small unit of the Pennsylvania Militia, and believed that, if needed, the men he had sent was more than enough to wipe out the unit. It was only when the two divisions off the army of Northern Virginia that the commanders had sent were suddenly face-to-face with what they believed was a small cavalry unit that they realized they were actually part of the Army of the Potomac, which was just a few leagues away from their position.

Upon the two units seeing each other, both sides opened fire and engaged each other's enemy. One of the cavalry men from the army of Northern Virginia was ordered to go back to their camp and request for reinforcements. It is at this point that the Battle of Gettysburg had officially begun.

Fun Fact:

There were about 384 battles that took place during the American Civil War that the United States Government had deemed significant enough to have made some kind of major impact in the progress of the American Civil War. However, many of these battlefields that should have been preserved landmarks, had been bought and converted into public spaces such as shopping malls, recreational spaces, and housing developments.

Fun Fact:

Though General Ulysses S. Grant and General Robert E. Lee fought on opposing sides during the American Civil War, they, actually, had both served in the army together during the Mexican War. Robert Lee served as the Chief of Staff of General Winfield Scott. Ulysses S. Grant, on the other hand, served as a quartermaster under the regiment of General Zachary Taylor.

Fill in the Blanks to Complete the Story

The generals of the army of ___________________ were convinced that the cavalry that was spotted was only a small unit of the ___________________, and believed that, if needed, the men he had sent was more than enough to wipe out the unit. It was only when the two divisions off the army of Northern Virginia that the commanders had sent were suddenly face-to-face with what they believed was a small cavalry unit that they realized they were actually part of the ___________________ which was just a few leagues away from their position.

Upon the two units seeing each other, both sides opened fire and engaged each other's enemy. One of the cavalry men from the army of Northern Virginia was ordered to go back to their camp and request for _______________. It is at this point that the _________________ had officially begun.

Answer:

The generals of the army of **Northern Virginia** were convinced that the cavalry that was spotted was only a small unit of the **Pennsylvania Militia,** and believed that, if needed, the men he had sent was more than enough to wipe out the unit. It was only when the two divisions off the army of Northern Virginia that the commanders had sent were suddenly face-to-face with what they believed was a small cavalry unit that they realized they were actually part of the **Army of the Potomac,** which was just a few leagues away from their position.

Upon the two units seeing each other, both sides opened fire and engaged each other's enemy. One of the cavalry men from the army of Northern Virginia was ordered to go back to their camp and request for **reinforcements**. It is at this point that the **Battle of Gettysburg** had officially begun.

DAY 1 OF THE BATTLE OF GETTYSBURG

The battle of the first day started the moment the two warring sides bumped into each other on the outskirts of Gettysburg. By the afternoon of that same day, the 11th Corps of the Union arrived to help bolster their defenses. The Confederates also had additional troops come in to help. Two Confederate divisions joined the battle from the northern side of Gettysburg, making a total of seventeen Confederate brigades present in the battle of the first day. The whole Confederate army currently fighting in Gettysburg was built with the strength of about twenty-seven thousand men. The Union, on the other hand, currently had only twenty-two thousand troops fighting for them in Gettysburg.

Though the gap in numbers actually is not that big of a difference, the soldiers fighting in the Union front have been spread out through all over the different areas of Gettysburg that was being used as a battlefield, and though the presence of the 11th corps was a great help, the members of which were all stretched too thin throughout the northern front. Their numbers were already small as it was compared to that of the Confederate soldiers, so it definitely was not in their favor that the position they were put in, were vulnerable to attacks from the Confederate soldiers. By the middle of the afternoon of that same day, the Union forces, more specifically, the 11th Corps, have been completely overwhelmed by the forces of the Confederate soldiers. Soon after the 11th Corps were overwhelmed, the collapse of the entire Union front line soon followed.

The Union troops were forced to flee on foot through the streets of Gettysburg with the troops of the Confederate Army right behind chasing them. Some Union troops had also decided to do a fighting retreat from the battlefield. Though they withdrew contact, they still took heavy casualty as the Confederate soldiers continued to shoot at them, though this decision helped the Union soldiers who had fled into the town to scatter and hide through the town.

The Confederacy had the Union Troops running and hiding, yet the generals of the Confederate troops made the decision to have the Confederate troops fall back and wait for more reinforcements to assist in the battle. While the Confederate troops were doing this, the Union soldiers went on the defensive and positioned themselves somewhere south of Gettysburg, which was the most defensible position in the area.

The first day of battle saw over fifteen thousand casualties, however, the number of casualties on this first day is nothing compared to the number of casualties that is still to come on the second and third day of the Battle of Gettysburg. Even though the Union soldiers were the ones who made the first move to withdraw, the reason why the Commanders of the Confederacy chose to not pursue, was because the Union still managed to defeat and injure many of their soldiers. This had marked the end of the battle for the first day. Both sides have decided it would be best to pause the fighting and regroup so that the battle may presume fresh the next day.

Fun Fact:

General Ulysses S. Grant was one of the best and top generals that served the Union during the American Civil War. However, despite his great prowess on the battlefield, the same could not be said for his time serving in office. In 1869, he was elected as the eighteenth President of the United States of America. He was actually thought to be one of the worst presidents the United States ever had.

Fun Fact:

After the war ended, General Robert E. Lee made no action to take back his Virginian estate, Arlington. His oldest son, George Washington Custis Lee, however, sued the government for taking Arlington illegally. The government agreed and gave the land back to him, complete with all the corpses of soldiers that had already buried in the land. Because they did not want to own land with hundreds, if not thousands, of corpses, the Lees sold Arlington back to the government, and then Arlington was later officially named, "Arlington National Cemetery."

Question:

1. What was Ulysses S. Grant during the American Civil War? What did he later become in 1869?

2. Why did the Lees sell Arlington back to the government?

3. Why was the soldiers of the 11th Corps initially easily overwhelmed?

4. Despite having a greater advantage in the moment, why were the Confederate soldiers ordered to retreat after the Union army retreated?

5. Why did General Robert E. Lee decide to retreat and wait instead of attacking after the Union retreated?

Answers:

1. General. President.

2. The Lees sold Arlington back to the government because of all the bodies already buried there.

3. The soldiers of the 11th Corps were initially easily overwhelmed because they were spread too thin across the battlefields.

4. The Confederate soldiers were ordered to make a retreat because General Robert Lee decided to wait for more of their reinforcements to arrive.

5. General Robert E. Lee decided to do this because many of the Confederate soldiers were also either defeated or heavily injured.

DAY 2 OF THE BATTLE OF GETTYSBURG

Before the battle began on July 2, 1863, the Army of the Potomac wasted no time in using their placement to their advantage for the upcoming fight. They had utilized the elevated terrain of Cemetery Hill to form a strong, compact, defensive line around the perimeter of their safe territory that consists of the majority of their armed forces. Other forces of the Army of the Potomac had established their positions in Culp's Hill to secure their right and left flanks respectively.

By midmorning of that day, the bulk of both of the armies had arrived to give aid and assistance to their respective comrades. Included in the additional forces that had arrived, six out of seven units of the Union Corps had also arrived to give assistance to the Army of the Potomac. The arrival of the six units of the Union Corps brings the total number of men fighting for the Union to sixty-nine thousand strong.

Major General George Meade had the Army of the Potomac and the Union Corps deployed the available units into specific areas around Gettysburg in order to create the shape of a fishhook, making the terrain they were occupying perfect for defense. The position of the Union Army was formed in the middle of Culp's Hill, going down to the western side of Cemetery Ridge. This decision was made in order to make give General Lee and his fifty-seven thousand men.

General Lee had some of his men attack the Union Army on Culp's Hill. This was a diversion, so that another troop could attack the majority of the Union Army, who were all positioned at the center of the fishhook formation. And finally, General Lee had his remaining forces attack the Union Army from the tail end of the fishhook, cutting off the supply chain of the Union Army.

The entire second day of the Battle of Gettysburg consisted of multiple battles in multiple areas around Gettysburg. There was a battle on Culp's Hill, Cemetery Ridge, Little Round Top, Big Round Top, and the Peach Orchard. The day started with the Union taking major hits from every direction, quickly being overpowered by the forces of the Confederate Army. However, in a quick turn of events, more reinforcements arrived, giving them the extra manpower that they needed so that they could push back against the Confederate Army.

The battles of the second day lasted long until nightfall. Though the Union Army started the day nearly being defeated, they ended the day still holding most of their lines. Though they had to lose the lower side of Culp's Hill, they were able to keep the rest of their defenses and positions. However, the cost of that day's win were the lives of ten thousand soldiers of their army.

The Confederate Army, however, only lost a total of seven thousand men. Though they did not suffer as many losses as the Union Army did, General Lee knew that there was now almost no hope of defeating the Army of the Potomac. Though they had more forces than the Union, and though the Union took great hits, the strength of the Union Troops seemed to him that it would be more than enough to defeat his own army.

Fun Fact:

The decision Major General George Meade made to have his men all form the shape of a fishhook in order to create a better defensive position was actually not really that of an issue for General Lee. General Lee was actually better at strategizing more on the offensive side of battle tactics, rather than on the defensive side. The Union being ordered to remain static had actually been more of an advantage for General Lee and his strategizing skills.

Fun Fact:

General Lee's plan of attacking the Union from multiple areas while the Union was on the defensive, should have been doomed to fail from the very beginning. The information he was given when forming that strategy was actually incorrect, and thus, would have failed. What made his plan almost succeed, however, was that General Daniel Sickles, the Commander of the third Union Corps, decided at the last minute that his men should position themselves in the middle of the Peach Orchard in order to gain higher ground. He was unaware, however, that General Lee's men were heading directly into that direction.

Match the General and Army to Their Correct Side

1. Union

2. Confederacy

Options: Major General Meade, General Robert E. Lee, Army of the Potomac, Army of Northern Virginia

Answers:

1. **Union:** Major General Meade, Army of the Potomac
2. **Hesiod:** General Robert E. Lee, Army of Northern Virginia

DAY 3 OF THE BATTLE OF GETTYSBURG

Still weakened and bloody from the previous day's battles, both the Union Army and the Confederate Army decided that they would keep their previous positions and strategies. The night before, after the battles of the second day, General Lee had ordered that when morning comes, his men shall keep attacking the already weakened left flank of the Union Army and to continue fighting for Culp's Hill.

General Lee's plans never made it to fruition. Before the battle even started, the Union Army had attacked the Confederate Army's camp on Culp's Hill with a heavy artillery barrage that was followed by an infantry assault, catching them by surprise as early as the crack of dawn. This battle to take over the position of Culp's Hill lasted seven hours straight. This was the longest struggle for a single position in the entire American Civil War. At the end of those seven hours, the Union came out victorious and succeeded in fully retaking Culp's Hill, forcing the Confederate troops to retreat and regroup.

General Lee's next plan was to attack the Union's rear and cut off their supply chain. He had General James Ewell Brown (J.E.B.) Stuart's cavalry division circle around in order to attack the Union rear from the east. However, the Union was ready for this sort of attack and was expecting it. The Union division led by General David Gregg was ready to meet the Confederate Army and defend the Union's rear. The Confederate Army attacked the rear with over a hundred and fifty cannons firing, while the Union fought back with over eighty Union guns in a firing barrage. This went on until General Stuart's division is forced to retreat.

On the other side of the battlefield, in the East, the infantry and cavalry of both armies went head-to-head. The battle escalated from skirmishes to full-blown charges and counter charges from both the Union and the Confederacy. Neither side of the war gained an advantage over the other.

General Lee makes one last attempt at gaining a victory

over the Union during the Battle of Gettysburg. At 2PM of that same day, after the retreat from Cemetery Ridge, Cemetery Hill and Little Round Top were the next two battlefields in Gettysburg. The Confederate troops continue their march towards the ridge line that the Army of the Potomac were defending. At the last moment, the Confederate soldiers were ordered to charge at the Union units stationed to defend Cemetery Ridge. The Confederates manage to break the defense that the Union had, but only for a moment. More Union Reinforcements arrived at the last minute to help defend the line and taking it back from the Confederate Army. The Confederate Army are forced to make another retreat as they were overpowered by the Union. The retreat marks General Lee's and the Confederate Army's failure.

The Confederate Army worried that the Army of the Potomac would go after them as they retreated, but thankfully, for their sake, the Army of the Potomac's forces were just as exhausted as they were, and thus, no offensive attack was made. This marked the end of the third and final day of the Battle of Gettysburg.

Fun Fact:

The reason why the Union Army, specifically General David Gregg's unit, was ready for a rear attack was because General J.E.B. Stuart had fired off four cannons in rapid succession in order to signal to General Lee that he and his unit were already in position and ready to go. The cannon firing did indeed signal to General Lee that they were ready, but in doing so, it had also signaled the Union Army as to where they were about to come from. Many have stated that General Stuart's actions were foolish and was what led to the loss of that part of the battle.

Fun Fact:

The firing of over a hundred fifty cannons from the Confederate Army combined with the firing of over eighty guns from the Union Army was the largest artillery bombardment of the American Civil War. This even was also considered as one of the loudest manmade noises in history up to that point.

True or False:

1. General Lee ordered his men to keep fighting even though night had already fallen.

2. the Union Army had attacked the Confederate Army's camp on Culp's Hill with a heavy artillery barrage.

3. The battle to take over the position of Culp's Hill lasted twenty-four hours straight.

4. The Confederate Army managed to break the defenses of the Union Army defending Cemetery Ridge but faltered when Union reinforcements arrived.

5. The Army of the Potomac continued to attack the Confederate Army instead of making a retreat to mark the end of the third day of battle.

Answers:

1. False. General Lee ordered his men to retreat and regroup, but gave instructions to keep the battle plans of the second day.

2. True.

3. False. The battle for Culp's Hill lasted only seven hours.

4. True.

5. False. When the Confederate Army retreated, the Army of the Potomac also retreated, which officially marked the end of the third day of battle.

THE FINAL RETREAT AND CHASE

The photo shows the Mississippi State Monument in Gettysburg National Park in Gettysburg, Pennsylvania. The statue depicts two soldiers in the heat of battle during the second day of the Battle at Gettysburg as the Mississippi brigade charge towards the Peach Orchard.

The morning after the third day of the Battle of Gettysburg, General Stuart had led some of the Confederate soldiers, specifically the Army of Northern Virginia, away to sneak off from the territory of and around Gettysburg. They had put their remaining supplies and their wounded soldiers into multiple wagons, making a train of them as they fled northwest before making its way south through the Cumberland Valley. As General Stuart led the Army of Northern Virginia and the supply train to safety, they were all being chased by a single Union Cavalry Troop.

The rest of the Confederate Army retreat towards the southwest. Among the Confederate troops fleeing to the southwest were the Confederate Third Corps that was being led by General Ambrose Powell Hill Jr., the Confederate First Corps that was being led by General James Longstreet, and the Confederate Second Corps that was being led by General James Ewell.

These Confederate Army soldiers fleeing southwest were being trailed by majority of the Union troops. Among the Union Army troops chasing after the rest of the Confederate Army soldiers were at least two Union Cavalries were the Sixth Corps that was being led by General John Sedgwick, the First Corps that were being led by General John Newton, the Third Corps that was being led by General William Henry French, the Fifth Corps that was being led by General George Sykes, the Eleventh Corps that was being led by General Oliver Otis Howard, the Second Corps that was being led by General Alexander Hays, and the Twelfth Corps that was being led by General Henry Warner Slocum.

Though the Confederate Army retreated in two different

directions, the Army of Northern Virginia led by General Stuart, and the bulk of the rest of the Confederate Army being led by General Ambrose Powell Hill Jr., General James Longstreet, and General James Ewell, all met at a single point: the territory of Virginia. Because Virginia is a state tied together with the Confederate Army, going into Virginia would not be a wise decision for the Union troops as they are most likely to be overpowered and defeated should they decide to push forward in their pursuit. The moment the Confederate Army entered Virginian territory, the Battle of Gettysburg had ended.

No battle had actually happened on the day of retreat – only a desperate pursuit. However, at the same day this was happening, all the way in Mississippi, what is later known as the "Siege of Vicksburg" was happening. The Confederate garrison troops stationed at the Fortress of Vicksburg had surrendered to General Ulysses S. Grant. The events of the Battle of Gettysburg and the Siege of Vicksburg happening simultaneously marked a very important point in the Civil War. Known as one of the deadliest battles of the American Civil War, the Battle of Gettysburg was the turning point. The

Confederate Army had never really been able to recover the losses that they had suffered on the early days of July of 1863, and thus never seriously threatened the Union ever again.

Fun Fact:

The Battle of Gettysburg had the most number of casualties in a single battle in the American Civil War. A total of about fifty-one thousand soldiers from both the Union Army and the Confederate army combined had perished during the three-day battle at Gettysburg. This is also known as the costliest and deadliest battle of the entire American Civil War.

Fun Fact:

The Battle of Gettysburg had the most number of generals who died in a battle with both the Union and the Confederacy combined. The ones who died on the Union side were Generals John Reynolds, Samuel Zook, Steven Weed, and Elon Farnsworth. On the Confederacy side, the ones who died were Generals Paul Jones Semmes, William Barksdale, William D. Pender, Richard Garnett, and Lewis Armistead.

Circle the Correct Word

1. General Stuart/Lee led the train of supply wagons to safety.

2. The majority of the Confederate Army fled northwest/southwest.

3. The Confederacy retreated to the territory of Virginia/Georgia.

4. General Ulysses S. Grant fought at the Battle of Gettysburg/Siege of Vicksburg.

5. The Battle of Gettysburg had the least/most number of casualties in a single battle in the American Civil War

Answers

1. General **Stuart** led the train of supply wagons to safety.

2. The majority of the Confederate Army fled **southwest**.

3. The Confederacy retreated to the territory of **Virginia**.

4. General Ulysses S. Grant fought at the **Siege of Vicksburg.**

5. The Battle of Gettysburg had the **most** number of casualties in a single battle in the American Civil War.

THE GETTYSBURG ADDRESS

The photo shows the Memorial of Abraham Lincoln and the text displayed behind the statue of him. This is located in Washington, D.C.

The Battle of Gettysburg took place on July 1st until July 3rd of 1863, with an immediate retreat to safety taking place on July 4th. After the Battle of Gettysburg, a dedicated cemetery for the Union soldiers who died at the Battle of Gettysburg was put in place by the Union government. The cemetery is called, Gettysburg National Cemetery. The cemetery is in Gettysburg, Pennsylvania, right where the battle took place.

Months later, on November 19, 1863, a dedication at the Gettysburg National Cemetery for those who fought and died at the Battle of Gettysburg took place. During that dedication, President Abraham Lincoln gave a two-minute speech that had become famously known as the "Gettysburg Address." The speech that President Abraham Lincoln gave was, again, only two minutes long, and had only consisted of about two hundred and seventy-two words. The speech was, by all accounts, considered short. Yet, despite its length, the Gettysburg Address was so impactful that it changed the rest of the Civil War and is said to be a way of guidance for people today.

In two hundred and seventy-two words, President Abraham Lincoln had manage to change the outlook that most people had about the American Civil War. The American Civil War is indeed a war between "North and South," "Union and Confederates," but it was also more than just about the people who were fighting in it. It was about what they were fighting for. It was not just a battle of the government versus the rebels. It was mainly about America being the center point of the universal struggle between the forces of tyranny and democracy, which again all goes back to the topic of slavery.

During his speech, President Abraham Lincoln managed to remind the people present at the dedication, and anyone else later on who heard about the speech, what America and its founding fathers envisioned for their country and its future. It reminded them that America's mission was to champion for liberty, equality, and freedom at every turn. In his speech, President Abraham Lincoln had also used words and phrases that were familiar to Christians in order to make it as simple and understandable for the common man, thus making such a valuable impact.

Initially, those who were actually present at the dedication and heard the speech firsthand did not really find anything that special about the Gettysburg Address. It was when President Lincoln's speech was transcribed and published later on that it became as special as it was. Union troops who read the transcription of the Gettysburg address were so inspired by President Lincoln's words that they fought so much harder for their victory in the American Civil War.

At the end of the American Civil War in April of 1865, Charles Sumner, an American statesman and then later a senator representing the Mississippi, stated that President Abraham Lincoln's "Gettysburg Address" actually did more for the American Civil War than the actual Battle of Gettysburg did.

Fun Fact:

President Abraham Lincoln had delivered the speech that had later become known as the "Gettysburg Address" in dedication to the Union soldiers who fought and died at the Battle of Gettysburg. Yet, years later, the Gettysburg Address had become so impactful that when it reached foreign countries, it even improved the foreign relationships that America had with other countries.

Fun Fact:

"The American Experiment" was the idea of the democratic principle of equal rights, general suffrage, and government. These were written by Thomas Jefferson and the other Founding Fathers in 1776 in the Declaration of Independence. In his speech at the dedication for the soldiers who perished at the Battle of Gettysburg, President Abraham Lincoln included words and phrases describing the American Experiment. It is said that most people have come to associate the ideas of the American Experiment with the Gettysburg Address rather than with the Declaration of Independence.

Reflection Questions

1. They say that the Gettysburg Address was so impactful that it is even used as a way of guidance for people today. Do you see any truth to this statement? Why or why not?

2. Charles Sumner stated that the Gettysburg Address did more for the American Civil War than the actual Battle of Gettysburg did. Do you believe that words might have been a more effective way to make one see reason than with violence? Why or why not?

THE END OF THE AMERICAN CIVIL WAR

The photo shows the entrance to the prisoner-of-war camp for captured Confederate soldiers in Johnson's Island in Sandusky Bay. Though about 15,000 men were incarcerated there, it is now filled with beautiful million dollar homes lining the shores.

Abraham Lincoln was reelected to be the President of the United States of America during the elections of 1864. Many people, specifically the Confederacy, were not happy about this turnabout at all. As the American Civil War seemed to be slowing down and drawing to a close, reelected President Abraham Lincoln now did not just have to worry about the divided country he had to lead yet again, but also whether or not the Confederacy, who were also referred to as, "the Rebel

Army" should be treated with any leniency for their actions that led up to, and during, the American Civil War.

This was then addressed during President Abraham Lincoln's (second) Inaugural Speech that he had delivered on March 4th, 1865. In his Inaugural Address, he stated his wish for the American Civil War to come to its end, and urged the Union and anyone else who fought against the Confederacy to forgive them and allow the country to become reunited so that the country may live on in peace.

Later that same month, President Abraham Lincoln had met with General Ulysses S. Grant, General William T. Sherman, and Admirable David Dickson Porter. They had a meeting about how they could end the American Civil War once and for all, and in that same meeting, President Abraham Lincoln stated that he planned to not give the Confederacy any punishment, as long as they agree to give up and allow the country to reunite. President Lincoln instructed his generals to offer lenient terms of surrender to the Confederate soldiers, specifying that they are welcome to return to their homes and no punishment will be given to them.

On April 1st, 1865, the Confederate strongholds of Petersburg in Richmond fell. This was important to the Confederate Army because the strongholds were their main source of supplies and was a strategic stronghold because it had five railroad lines connected to it and other major roads that would lead to their other territories. Petersburg was mainly responsible for the supplies given to the army of General Robert Lee.

On April 9th, 1865, General Robert Lee finally surrendered the Army of Northern Virginia to General Ulysses S. Grant at a courthouse in Virginia. On April 26, General Joseph E. Johnson surrendered his troops to General Sherman in North Carolina. With the surrender of the two major generals of the Confederate Army, the American Civil War was officially over.

Unfortunately, President Abraham Lincoln never got to see the actual end of the American Civil War because, on April 14, 1865, he had attended a play with his wife and was assassinated in the theater by John Wilkes Booth, an actor and Confederate supporter. He died the following morning after being shot to the head.

General Ulysses S. Grant, General William T. Sherman, and Admirable David Dickson Porter all respected President Abraham Lincoln's final wishes and made sure that the former Confederate soldiers would be left unpunished and would even be allowed to go back to working for the American government.

Fun Fact:

he Union Army was a mix of American soldiers, immigrants, and former African slaves. Some of the nationalities of those who fought for the Union were, French, Italian, Polish, English, and Scottish. There were so many foreigners fighting in the Union to the point that some regiments were built up almost entirely of foreigners.

Fun Fact:

For a time during the American Civil War, Black Union soldiers were being paid lower wages than White Union soldiers. Because of this, Black Union soldiers refused to accept their wages for eighteen months as a form of protest because they thought that the difference in wages only because they had different skin colors and because they were former slaves was an unfair justification for the difference.

Reflection Questions

1. Abraham Lincoln wanted to end the war and promised leniency to the Confederacy once the war ends. If leniency was never on the table and Abraham Lincoln pursued the Confederacy with violence, would the Civil War had gone on for much longer than it did?

2. After Abraham Lincoln died, his generals honored his wishes to grant leniency to those who were apart of the Confederacy. How differently would the Civil War had ended had the generals decided to ignore Lincoln's final command since he was dead?

CONCLUSION

"Those dead shall not have died in vain."

– Abraham Lincoln (The Gettysburg Address)

It is easy to read the accounts of what happened during the Battle of Gettysburg and easily get lost in the details of every single decision the generals made, in every troop of each side that came to assist their fellow soldiers, it is even easy to get lost scanning the maps of Gettysburg, plotting out every move the Union Army and the Confederate Army made and the battles they fought in each and every area of Gettysburg.

Cemetery Ridge, Culp's Hill, Little Round Top, Big Round Top, even the Peach Orchard was not spared from the blood shed that took place in Gettysburg, Pennsylvania. For three days hundreds of thousands of men fought for their lives, their beliefs, and their futures. Again, a battle that started on pure coincidence lasted three days and has been recorded in history as the deadliest battle of the entire American Civil War.

Over a century later, this is the battle that almost everyone who only has very minimal knowledge about the American Civil War connects to it. It was so famous and so deadly that many at least know it by its name, if not any details about it. Yet, with how much of an impact it had in the American Civil War, the war itself did not end until almost two years later in 1865. Once the war ended and the United States recovered from the losses and destruction caused by the Civil War, monuments and memorials were being built to commemorate the lives that fought valiantly and were lost to battle.

Today, many of these sites that were made to memorialize the lives of those who perished in the war, are still visited and paid respects to by many. The American Civil War was one of the deadliest and costliest in the most recent centuries, yet the result of the Civil War changed the lives of many for the better.

Discussion Question:

1. One of the main conflicts that started the American Civil War was whether slavery should be abolished. The Union wanted to abolish slavery, whilst the Confederacy wanted to keep it. Do you think a war was necessary, or could peace talks and discussions have sufficed?

2. The Union always had the higher advantage during the Civil War. The Union had majority of the states on their side, a full functioning government, and majority of the country's supply and resources. Do you think the war would have ended differently had the Confederacy been the one with all these advantages?

3. Most of the people who fought for the Union side were volunteers and were willing to fight because they believed in the cause. The Confederacy also had many people willing to fight for them, but a lot of their soldiers were also slaves who were forced to be there. Do you think the position and circumstances of the soldiers affected the outcome of the battles and, in turn, the war?

4. The Battle of Gettysburg happened only because an army

from each side just happened to run into each other by chance. The battle officially started when the Confederacy called for reinforcements and turned it into a full-scale battle. If these two armies had not run into each other, do you think Gettysburg would have still eventually become a battlefield during the Civil War?

5. On the morning of the third day of battle, the Union caught the Confederacy by surprise when they suddenly attacked them with a heavy artillery barrage that was followed by an infantry assault. This surprise attack allowed the Union to gain the upper hand in the Battle of Gettysburg. Do you think a surprise attack like this was fair?

6. After three days straight of fighting, the Confederacy decide to make a retreat into the safety of Virginia. The Union pursued them in hopes of engaging them in another battle. Had the Confederacy not decided to make a retreat, do you think the Battle of Gettysburg would have lasted longer than the three days that it did?

7. During the dedication of the memorial for the Union

soldiers who died at Gettysburg, President Abraham Lincoln delivered a speech that inspired a nation. The speech he gave was so impactful that it was later named, the Gettysburg Address and was said to have been a major turning point in the war in favor to the Union. How different do you think the latter half of the Civil War could have turned out had President Abraham Lincoln not deliver such an effective speech?

8. During his second inaugural speech, President Lincoln already stated that those involved in the Confederacy would have been granted leniency, no matter what. He spoke with his generals and had them offer these terms to the Confederate generals who then decided to surrender instead of prolonging the war. Knowing they would have been granted leniency anyway, do you think there was a possibility that they would not have surrendered and continue fighting instead?

True/False Questions

1. True or False: Slavery started in America in 1526. During the 19th century, many wanted to abolish slavery. Slavery was one of the main issues of conflict that started the American Civil War. The side that wanted to keep slavery was called the Confederacy.

2. True or False: President Abraham Lincoln was against abolishing slavery. He led the Union side and had them fight to keep slavery. Many slaves fought for the Union.

3. True or False: The American Civil War officially started in 1861 when the Confederacy opened fire in Fort Sumter. Fort Sumter was, prior to the Civil War, under the jurisdiction of the Union, but was in South Carolina, a Confederate State. Fort Sumter was crucial territory to the Union's Cause.

4. True or False: The Battle of Gettysburg started when the Confederate Army and the Union Army chanced upon each other in Gettysburg, Pennsylvania. A few Confederate soldiers had actually seen some Union Army soldiers in town and reported back to their

superiors. General Robert Lee sent his men off to collect intelligence about the Union troop they saw, not realizing they were only a portion of the Army of the Potomac just nearby.

5. True or False: The Battle of Gettysburg was a whole planned out affair. General Robert Lee knew the Army of the Potomac would be in Pennsylvania, so he brought his forces there to engage in conflict with them. The Confederacy was prepared beforehand to fight at Gettysburg.

6. True or False: General Robert Lee and General Ulysses S. Grant served in the Mexican War together. This was years before they were named "general" of their respective factions. They later became the top generals within the side they were fighting for.

7. True or False: The speech Abraham Lincoln delivered at the dedication for the cemetery dedicated to the Union soldiers who died at the Battle of Gettysburg was so uninspiring and forgettable. The speech was dubbed "The Gettysburg Address" out of mockery for how terrible it was. To this day, people still find the

Gettysburg Address to be useless and humorous only.

8. True or False: Abraham Lincoln was reelected to be the President of the United States. In his second inaugural speech, he expressed his wish for the war to end and even promised leniency to those who fought for the Confederacy. Upon his death, his major generals respected his wishes and assured General Robert Lee and many of his comrades leniency.

True/False Answers:

1. True.

2. False. President Abraham Lincoln wanted to end slavery. The Union fought to abolish slavery, and had former slaves to fight for the Union.

3. True.

4. True.

5. False. General Robert Lee and his men were in Pennsylvania not knowing the Army of the Potomac would be just nearby. The two armies only met in pure coincidence and then engaged in conflict.

6. True.

7. False. The Gettysburg Address, though it had no impact to those who were able to hear it first hand, was later transcribed and circulated around, becoming one of the most inspiring speeches in history. It is believed that the Gettysburg Address was even more of a turning point than the actual Battle of Gettysburg was.

8. True.

BIBLIOGRAPHY

- The photograph shows an aerial view of a battle reenactment of the Battle of Gettysburg. This photograph was taken in 1922.
  "Aerial View of Battle Reenactment, Gettysburg, 1922" by Archives Branch, USMC History Division is licensed under CC BY 2.0. To view a copy of this license, visit https://creativecommons.org/licenses/by/2.0/?ref=openverse.
- The picture is a picture of a painting from the cyclorama of the Battle of Gettysburg.
  "Photo from the Paintings of the Cyclorama of the Battle of Gettysburg" by tornintwo2011 is licensed under CC BY 2.0. To view a copy of this license, visit https://creativecommons.org/licenses/by/2.0/?ref=openverse
- The photo is a picture of the 105th Wildcats Regiment Memorial of the Battle of Gettysburg. This is located in the outer corner of the Peach Orchard that was also used as a battlefield during the Battle of Gettysburg.
  "File:PA 105th Wildcats Regiment Battle of Gettysburg Memorial.jpg" by Bryandgeer is licensed under CC BY-SA 3.0. To view a copy of this license, visit https://creativecommons.org/licenses/by-sa/3.0/?ref=openverse.
- The photo shows Confederate prisoners after the Battle of Gettysburg that was taken in 1863. This photo was originally in black and white, but was later colorized.
  "Confederate Prisoners After the Battle of Gettysburg, 1862, Colorized" by lisby1 is marked with Public Domain Mark 1.0. To view the terms, visit https://creativecommons.org/publicdomain/mark/1.0/?ref=openverse.

- The photo shows the Memorial of Abraham Lincoln and the text displayed behind the statue of him. This is located in Washington, D.C.
  "Happy 200th Birthday, Mr. Lincoln (Text of Gettysburg Address)" by Tony Fischer Photography is licensed under CC BY 2.0. To view a copy of this license, visit https://creativecommons.org/licenses/by/2.0/?ref=openverse.

- The photo shows the entrance to the prisoner-of-war camp for captured Confederate soldiers in Johnson's Island in Sandusky Bay. Though about 15,000 men were incarcerated there, it is now filled with beautiful million dollar homes lining the shores.
  "Johnson Island6" by Counselman Collection is licensed under CC BY-SA 2.0. To view a copy of this license, visit https://creativecommons.org/licenses/by-sa/2.0/?ref=openverse.

- The photo shows the Mississippi State Monument in Gettysburg National Park in Gettysburg, Pennsylvania. The statue depicts two soldiers in the heat of battle during the second day of the Battle at Gettysburg as the Mississippi brigade charge towards the Peach Orchard.
  "Mississippi State Monument -- Seminary Ridge Gettysburg National Military Park (PA) April 2012" by Ron Cogswell is licensed under CC BY 2.0. To view a copy of this license, visit https://creativecommons.org/licenses/by/2.0/?ref=openverse.

About Us

At our core, we believe that history is more than just a subject to be learned. It's an experience to be had.

Our mission is to educate and inspire the next generation by providing them with a window into the fascinating and often surprising world of the past. We want to help young people make sense of the complexities of history and understand the lessons it has to offer.

By creating unforgettable encounters with relics of the past, we hope to ignite a lifelong passion for learning and discovery.

Thank you,